Daft Punk

by **Sarah Tieck**

Big Buddy Books
An Imprint of Abdo Publishing
www.abdopublishing.com

www.abdopublishing.com

Published by Abdo Publishing, a division of ABDO, PO Box 398166, Minneapolis, Minnesota 55439.
Copyright © 2015 by Abdo Consulting Group, Inc. International copyrights reserved in all countries. No part
of this book may be reproduced in any form without written permission from the publisher. Big Buddy Books™
is a trademark and logo of Abdo Publishing.

Printed in the United States of America, North Mankato, Minnesota.
092014
012015

**THIS BOOK CONTAINS
RECYCLED MATERIALS**

Cover Photo: Jordan Strauss/Invision/AP.
Interior Photos: AFP/Getty Images (pp. 17, 25); ASSOCIATED PRESS (pp. 7, 9, 21); Getty Images (p. 27); Getty
        Images for NARAS (p. 29); ©iStockphoto.com (p. 11); Frank Micelotta/Invision/AP (p. 20); Redferns (p. 15);
        Matt Sayles/Invision/AP (pp. 5, 19); Shutterstock.com (p. 13); WireImage (pp. 10, 23).

Coordinating Series Editor: Rochelle Baltzer
Contributing Editors: Bridget O'Brien, Marcia Zappa
Graphic Design: Maria Hosley

Library of Congress Cataloging-in-Publication Data

Tieck, Sarah, 1976- author.
  Daft Punk : electronic music duo / Sarah Tieck.
     pages cm. -- (Big buddy biographies)
  ISBN 978-1-62403-567-8
1. Daft Punk (Musical group)--Juvenile literature. 2. Alternative rock musicians--France--Biography--Juvenile litera-
ture. I. Title.
  ML3930.D254T54 2015
  782.42166092'2--dc23
  [B]
                            2014026414

Contents

The members of Daft Punk are known for their style and costumes.

Music Stars

Daft Punk is a popular **electronic music** group. Guy-Manuel de Homem-Christo and Thomas Bangalter make up Daft Punk. They have made award-winning albums.

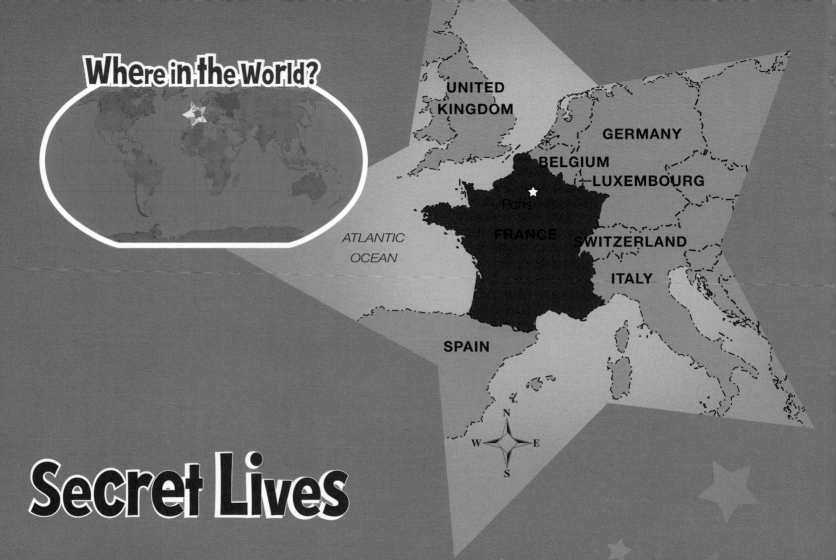

UNITED KINGDOM

GERMANY

BELGIUM

LUXEMBOURG

ATLANTIC OCEAN

Paris

FRANCE

SWITZERLAND

ITALY

SPAIN

N

W E

S

Secret Lives

The members of Daft Punk don't share much about their lives. Guy-Manuel is short for Guillaume Emmanuel. He was born on February 8, 1974, in Paris, France.

Did you know...

Guy-Manuel's great-grandfather was Portuguese writer Francisco Manuel Homem Cristo Filho.

Guy-Manuel (*front*) comes from a wealthy family. They ran an advertising agency in Paris.

Thomas was born on January 3, 1975, in Paris. His dad was a music producer. His mom was a ballet dancer.

Thomas's family was wealthy. His father wrote well-known disco songs. They had an effect on Thomas's musical taste and style.

Thomas (*front*) and Guy-Manuel have been friends since their school years.

School Years

Guy-Manuel and Thomas met in 1987. They attended the same school in Paris. Both boys were interested in music.

By 1992, the boys and another friend had formed a band called Darlin'. Thomas played bass and Guy-Manuel played guitar. Their friend Laurent Brancowitz played drums.

Paris is a famous city in Europe. The Eiffel Tower is a popular site to visit. Can you spot it?

Starting Out

Darlin' got bad reviews from **critics**. One writer said the group's music was "a daft punky thrash." He considered it silly rock music.

Before long, Darlin' broke up. But, Guy-Manuel and Thomas formed a new group in 1993. They called it Daft Punk. They recorded **electronic music**. Their first song was "The New Wave."

People use keyboard synthesizers (*above*) and drum machines (*below*) to make electronic music.

13

First Album

Guy-Manuel and Thomas continued to record music as Daft Punk. In 1997, they **released** their first album. It is called *Homework*. The songs "Da Funk" and "Around the World" became global hits.

In 2001, the duo released *Discovery*. "One More Time" was a hit around the world. "Digital Love" was also popular. Later that year, Daft Punk released a live album called *Alive 1997*.

Helmets became part of Daft Punk's look around 2001. Before that, they often wore Halloween masks.

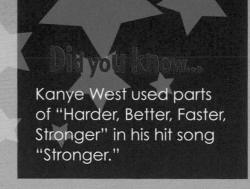

Did you know...

Kanye West used parts of "Harder, Better, Faster, Stronger" in his hit song "Stronger."

In 2005, Daft Punk put out a new album called *Human After All*. In 2007, Daft Punk **released** *Alive 2007*. One hit song was "Harder, Better, Faster, Stronger." It won a **Grammy Award** in 2009 for Best Dance Recording.

In 2010, Daft Punk put out an album for the movie *Tron: Legacy*. "Derezzed" was a popular song.

Daft Punk performed with Kanye West at the 2008 Grammy Awards.

Helmet Heads

Guy-Manuel and Thomas are known for wearing helmets when they **perform**. They also wear them at music and media events.

Daft Punk wants to create a show for the audience. Guy-Manuel and Thomas want people to think about the music instead of them. That is why they wear helmets.

Thomas (*left*) usually wears a silver helmet. Guy-Manuel (*right*) usually wears a gold helmet. Sometimes, they wear different helmets for special performances.

Hit Album

Daft Punk released *Random Access
Memories* in 2013. It was the group's
biggest hit yet! Popular songs are "Get
Lucky" and "Lose Yourself to Dance."

Random Access Memories

Daft Punk named *Random Access Memories* to compare people's brains to computer hard drives.

In 2014, "Get Lucky" won Grammy Awards for Record of the Year and Best Pop Duo/Group Performance.

In 2014, *Random Access Memories* won many awards. It received three Grammy Awards. One was Album of the Year! It was also recognized as Best Dance/Electronica Album and Best Engineered Album, Non-Classical.

Nile Rodgers, Pharrell Williams, Daft Punk, and Stevie Wonder (*left to right*) performed at the 2014 Grammy Awards.

A Musical Life

Guy-Manuel and Thomas spend time working on their music. They come up with ideas and work on new sounds. And, they go to recording studios to make albums.

After an album comes out, Daft Punk **promotes** it. They appear in magazines. And sometimes, they **perform** live for fans.

Fans around the world were excited for the launch of *Random Access Memories*.

Off the Stage

Because of their talent, Guy-Manuel and Thomas have become popular. They attend many events and have received special honors and awards.

Daft Punk uses its success to help others. Guy-Manuel and Thomas support causes they care about. In 2011, they sold a Ferrari to raise money for disaster relief in Japan.

In 2013, Guy-Manuel and Thomas wrote words to one of their songs on a skateboard. It was sold to raise money to build skate parks through the Tony Hawk Foundation.

27

Buzz

Guy-Manuel and Thomas continue to work hard and succeed as Daft Punk. In 2014, they put out a new song called "Computerized" with rapper Jay-Z. Fans look forward to seeing what's next for them!

Thomas (*left*) and Guy-Manuel (*right*) walked the red carpet before the 2014 Grammy Awards.

Snapshot

★**Names**: Guy-Manuel de Homem-Christo, Thomas Bangalter

★**Birthdays**: February 8, 1974 (Guy-Manuel); January 3, 1975 (Thomas)

★**Birthplaces**: Paris, France

★**Albums**: *Homework, Discovery, Alive 1997, Human After All, Alive 2007, Tron: Legacy, Random Access Memories*

Important Words

critic a person who has the job of giving opinions about music, theater, art, or books.

disco a type of music that first became popular in the 1970s. It includes elements of funk, Latin, and soul music.

electronic music popular music that uses technology, recordings, and electronic musical instruments.

Grammy Award any of the awards given each year by the National Academy of Recording Arts and Sciences. Grammy Awards honor the year's best accomplishments in music.

perform to do something in front of an audience.

producer a person who oversees the making of a movie, a play, an album, or a radio or television show.

promote to help something become known.

release to make available to the public.

Websites

To learn more about Big Buddy Biographies, visit **booklinks.abdopublishing.com**. These links are routinely monitored and updated to provide the most current information available.

Index